Health Through New Thought and Fasting

by Wallace D. Wattles

Originally published in 1907.

CONTENTS:

Commentary by Elizabeth Towne:

"Starve and be a Samson!"

That is the first line of an illustrated article in a recent number of the New York World, wherein are described the wonderful feats of Gilman Low who "lifted 1,000,000 pounds in thirty-five minutes." When he finds a car track obstructed by a disabled auto, Gilman Low lifts the 1,500 pound touring car out of the way as easily as you or I might move a baby wagon.

Gilman Low has broken all sorts of athletic records, but not on accepted principles of training. Once before, after using conventional methods, three meals a day with meat, etc, he attempted that 1,000,000 pound lift, which consisted in getting under a 1,000 pound weight and raising it on his back 1,000 times in half an hour. That time he raised it 500 times in twenty-five minutes and had to quit.

This time he trained for the feat by living first five weeks on one meal a day, consisting of three eggs, half a loaf of whole wheat bread and raw fruit, nuts or cereals, with was glass of milk taken afterward. During the day he drank plenty of cool, distilled water. Twice during the period he ate meat, but found it detrimental and ceased using it. The three weeks he ate but four meals a week, of the foods before mentioned. At 10 a.m of the day the lift was made, he ate six eggs and plenty of bread.

During the eight weeks of training his exercise consisted principally of walking and deep breathing, combined with light gymnastics, and he kept out of doors as much as possible, being a firm believer in the benefits of fresh air and sunshine.

His 1,000,000 pound lifting was performed before a. medical examiner kind many witnesses,, When he had lifted the 1,000 pound weight 800 times his pulse registered only eighty-five, an increase of thirteen beats, showing a wonderful condition of heart and circulation. During the first one hundred lifts Low's arms were folded across his chest. After that his hands rested on a heavy bench and he lifted with arms, legs and back, increasing speed as he neared the close of his feat.

It cost Gilman Low exactly five and three-quarters pounds in the half-hour of lifting. And he prepared for it by living eight weeks on forty-seven meals, an average of one meal in over one and one-fifth days, And at only two of these meals he ate meat, finding afterwards that it interfered with his work.

When one thinks of Gilman Low eating air and lifting 1,000 pounds a thousand times in half an hour his imagination skips Samson as unimportant. Why not Atlas, standing on 'air, living on Mr and lifting the earth?

How much more can Gilman Low do by eliminating a few more meals? He has already performed wonders after seven to fifteen day fasts. During the physical culture show he fasted seven days and then with the back lift raised 2,000 pounds twenty-two times in nineteen seconds. What next?

All this goes to prove "The New Science of Living" as elucidated by 'Wallace D. Wattles in the the few chapters of this book.

One of our correspondents asks, "If food is not necessary to maintenance of the physical being, why do all fowls and animals eat nearly continuously? Why does a babe cry for food at frequent intervals, though it sleeps much of the time "

Nobody imagines that food is not "necessary to the maintenance of physical life." It is.

But food is not the source of physical power, as the old physiology teaches.

Food is to the body what raw material is to the builder. The power which receives food, dissolves and changes it, and builds it into muscle and tissue, nerves, and brain, is the Lift Power which flows into us from the Infinite while we sleep.

If we give this Life Power the right food materials, and the right amount of it, it builds beautifully, intelligently, ever improving and refining it work.

If we give too little food material this Life Power builder within us is hampered in its work, just as any carpenter would be if the mill failed to deliver the necessary lumber for the work planned. The body stores enough material for a forty, or fifty, or sixty day famine, but not enough for eternal famine. Not yet, at least.

If we give too much food material, or not the right kind, it is at if the lumber dealer kept delivering loads of all kinds of lumber until the premises were covered with it. Imagine carpenters trying to build a house in the center of a lumber yard, with all kinds of timber piled about and more coming in with every revolution of the saw, and you will get a faint idea of the difficulties under which labors the builder which is you, when you pour in more food material than he needs.

And the danger of pouring in too much food is far greater than that of delivering too little. For the reason that too much food sets up a state of general inflammation throughout the body, which you interpret as a call for more food, when in reality it means there is already too much on hand. A baby suffering from indigestion acts ravenous. A grown-up stomach that is generating ferments calls for more, more, And soother meal piled in gives temporary relief, just as kneading more flour into a batch of bread dough gives temporary relief from ferment.

What world happen to the dough if you kept on kneading it down with more flour, a dozen, a hundred, yes, thousands of times. The result would be unwieldiness and poison.. The same thing happens in the continuously overloaded stomach, and throughout the overloaded body.

And no amount of mental or spiritual science will stop it, though it may retard the process, as cold retards the rising of your bread dough.. In this way you may put off the day of reckoning with an overloaded stomach and body, but that is all you can do. The death-poison will get you sooner or later.

There is little danger of giving the builder within you too little material first, because the body of every person carries enough building material in storage to last a complete famine of thirty to sixty days, or more; second, because the normal hunger of an unstuffed and untempted body is an infallible guide to the amount and kind of food needed.

All our overeating comes from, first, the false belief that strength is gained from eating; second, the habit of eating so many times a day whether hungry or not; third, the continual tempting of the appetite through variety of diarrhea. Of course, the latter two causes are branches of the first.

The cure and the proof of the new physiology is to eat plain foods, cut out one meal a day, and take 36-hour fasts once a week for say four or five months. The improvement in feelings and endurance, and the change in appetite and tastes will prove the matter to all but the most hopelessly prejudiced minds.

Now, note that normal fowls hunt food "nearly continuously," but they come a long way from eating continuously. And the hunting and scratching enable them to make good use of all. food they can find.

Every poulterer knows that fowls penned up and overfed lay few eggs and suffer from numerous diseases.

And no animals come anywhere near eating "nearly continuously" except cattle, and they exercise while eating, and if they get over the fence into a too rich field they soon die of over-eating.

If you were to weigh the total amount a cow eats in a day, even in good pasturage, you would find she consumes less in proportion to her weight than the ordinary human being does. And she exercises nearly all the time and gives milk into the bargain.

Another correspondent takes exceptions to Mr. Wattle's statements: about fear and digestion, and cites the case of an old lady who "has always eaten much, and anything she wanted, and does yet; who knows nothing about chemistry of foods, consequently has no fear of results of eating; and yet she has been a victim to sick headache, nerves sad kindred troubles all her life,"

I should think so. Fear is not the only thing that causes such troubles. And fear of what one eats is not the only kind of fear that hinders digestion. The more fear of any kind one entertains the less food be can properly digest, for fear paralyzes digestive and other processes. Any fear.

But over-eating and wrong eating are at the bottom of all sick headaches. If one adds fear to over eating be suffers more and oftener, that's all. This same correspondent says she must have four meals a day, as she is "no good" with her stomach empty, and she can "work all around her daughter who eats half as much and sleeps twice as much,"

If she will cut her meals to two a day and fast thirty-six hours once a week, living thus, feelings or no feelings, for, say six weeks, doing it with a will, she will find herself doing still more work, with greater health and mental brightness than ever, and the gone feelings all gone for good. To merely assert that she must have four meals proves nothing. She will prove the opposite if she practices the new way.

And for one person to compare herself to another is futile. It proves nothing, for no two humans are alike. The daughter can cut her meals in two and fast one day a week, and she will doubtless do more work than at present, and require less sleep.

For over-eating is one great cause of over-sleeping. Any sort of bodily exercise, including digestion, places the demand for more sleep that the Life Power may accumulate energy to renew the broken down tissues. People of active living, like growing children, need much sleep. And people who eat much need much sleep, for it takes much Life Power to dispose of the food.

One person cannot be compared justly with another in such things; but one can try different methods of living, try them faithfully and prove which is best, thus measuring himself by himself. So far this correspondent seems to have tried only one sort of living.

To eat all one really needs and no more, because the elimination of unneeded food requires Life Power or energy that would better be directed in other channels --- this is the intent of the new physiology. Sensible, is it not?

--Elizabeth Towne

Chapter 1 - THE SOURCE OR WORK-POWER

Life passes through us, we do not possess it. ---Amiel

THE SOURCE OR WORK-POWER

IT IS PROBABLE that the late Edward Hooker Dewey M.D. of Meadville, Pa., widely known as "the no-breakfast doctor," influenced more people in the direction of the simplification of life than any other writer, living or dead. His books, "The New Science of Health," and "The No Breakfast Plan" have been read by many thousands of people and have indirectly influenced many thousands more; his theories are working a revolution, and yet scarcely one in ten of his followers comprehends the really revolutionary character of his thought, or the tremendous importance of his great physiological discovery.

In brief, as set forth in his last book, that discovery it this: That the strength --- the work-power --- of the human organism is not drawn from the food consumed but is renewed in sleep. The storage battery of muscle energy and thought energy is not charged and re-charged at the dining table, but in the bedroom. Food is to the human body what the soil is to a plant --- merely raw material.; tissue elements, to be built into the organism, but not in any sense a source of life.

The interesting points about this theory are:

First, that it is capable of mathematical demonstration, and is therefore true beyond controversy;

Second, that it absolutely overthrows current theories of the sours of life and strength, driving the materialistic physiologist from the field by proving that life energy is not the product of functional action, and that most muscle workers would be healthier, stronger and longer find on one-half, and most brain workers on one-tenth of the quantity of food they now consume. It gives good ground also for the argument that mind is not produced by the body, but that mind produces the body; that the brain does not produce thought, but that thought produces the brain; that there is no chemistry by which a piece of bread can become mind or thought;

Third, it proves that most of the conclusions of the pseudo-science of medicine have been based on false premises, and are erroneous; and that most of the sick are greatly hindered in recovery by feeding, dosing and other interference.

It gives us, also a solid foundation upon which we may base a really scientific investigation of the problems the origin of life, and of the immortality of the soul; but that is beyond the scope of this article.

Let us now "make good" on our first proposition: That we do not get our strength from food. The brain is a storage battery of vital energy, which it charged in. some unknown manner, and from some unknown source, during steep. The "stomach is a machine which is run by brain Power and the digestion of food is a tax on strength, and not a source of strength.

Now, as to the mathematics! A laborer will consume a beefsteak and a couple of potatoes, and will shovel twenty tons of earth to a height of five feet; was there sufficient potential energy in the food to perform the work. A Japanese soldier, carrying a heavy load, can march and fight all day and only consume a handful of rice; and be can do this for an indefinite period without loss of weight or strength.

Can any one seriously claim that the enormous amount of energy he displays was potentially in the few ounces at rice consumed per diem? No machine which science has been able to devise can extract one five-hundredth part as much energy from a pound of beef as the human body must draw from it if the old physiology is true', but it is not true, It is mathematically impossible. A man will eat a few slices of pork, and will "run down," catch and overpower two or three full grown hogs by the sheer excess of his physical power over theirs. Is the potential energy of a pound of dead pork greater than the kinetic energy of three live three hundred pound hogs. Consider next, the numerous cases of protracted fasts which have been recorded since Dr. Dewey's books were published.

Leonard Thress, of Philadelphia, fifty-six days, and Miss Estella Kuenzel, forty two days, with a steady gain in strength from the first day, are among the eases recorded by the doctor himself; and some hundreds of others, perfectly authenticated, prove that a person can go from twenty to sixty days without food and can often do so without appreciable loss of strength. I believe it is the accepted dictum of the old physiology that a man will starve to death in ten days. This has been proved to be a mistake, and it is evident that most of the people who have perished of hunger in that limited time died because they thought they had to, and that, property educated, they might have lived from twenty to sixty days longer. In death by starvation the brain and nervous system, which are the power plant, lose no weight; the other tissues disappear until the skeleton condition is reached, and death comes because the brain can get no more raw material with which to repair the heart, lungs, stomach, liver, etc. The organism grows weak and perishes from lack of raw material to replace the daily waste of its vital parts; it dies when the viscera are so attenuated as to be unable to perform their functions, but. it dies not for lack of vital energy, but because the vital. energy ban no material to use in keeping up the organism.. Set a plant. in gravel, and it will die --- not for lack of energy, but for lack of material.

Consider for a moment this claim that the body works with energy generated by its own digestive system. The digestion of food is certainly work, and it certainly takes power; those who remember the feeling of lethargy after a too hearty meal will not be disposed to deny that a very considerable amount of energy is required to operate the stomach. The old physiology claims that the heart, brain, liver, kidneys, etc., are machines which are operated by power which is ultimately traced to the action of the stomach; and that the stomach, in turn, is operated by power which is generated by the action of the heart, brain, liver, kidneys, etc. Here is a mechanical impossibility --- the stomach generating power to operate the other machines and being in turn operated by power supplied by the other machines. That the body should perform its great amount of external work by Means of energy generated by its own internal work is impossible; the claim that it does so is an absurdity. The functional actions of the Viscera do not generate energy; they absorb energy. It uses up power to spade up the earth in the garden; and the heart and stomach cannot generate power to operate themselves, with a sufficient surplus to spade up the garden also. It is, I repeat, an absurd denial of all known chemical and mechanical principles to assert that the body works by means of energy generated by its own functional action. As well claim that a man can lift himself by his boot straps.

Power is stored in the brain during sleep, and is probably transmitted to the muscles and organs over the nerves in a manner similar to the transmission of electrical energy over a trolley wire; and, there is no evidence that this power comes from our food at all. Food does not "strengthen" us; there is no such thing as a "strengthening" food. We need food to furnish the tissue elements, not to supply power; and every mouthful we eat in excess of the actual need weakens us and tends to shorten our lives. Most people expend more than half of their total life. force in the disposition of unnecessary food; if we only ate from one-tenth to one-half of what we now consume most of us would die of old age, and the average of life in the next generation would probably be beyond the century mark. This shocks you, doesn't it? Well, it is hard, scientific fact; I am just trying to write it in plain common sense words.

But you say, do not we feel more strength after eating! Yea, but not after digesting our food. If strength comes from the assimilation of food it can only be after the food is completely digested; a partially digested mass in the stomach certainly cannot yield any work power. Now it takes some hours, at least, to complete the process of assimilation; but the accession of strength is always felt immediately after swallowing the food. You are tired and weak; you swallow a cup of coffee and a piece of toast, and you rise and go to work refreshed; it has "strengthened" you, you say. But it has not; if you will pause to think you will see that your fresh strength cannot have come from the food, which has not had time to be changed at all; it is coffee and toast in your stomach, and will be, for some time; how can it strengthen you before it is digested? And three or four hours. hence, when it is digested, you will be as weak as ever. If we get our energy from food, is it before or after we digest it?

You are stronger right after your noon-day meal, but at five p.m. when the food is digested, you are all tired out; and with all your eating you suffer a steady decline in power from the time you emerge from unconsciousness in the morning until you. return to it at night. The accession of strength you felt after taking the coffee and toast did not come from the food; it was the rally nature made, summoning her power to the task of disposing of the food. She drew on the brain for an extra supply of its stored-up energy to perform the work of digestion, and as this power was turned on you felt it throughout the body; but the power came from the brain, and not from the stomach.

We do not live by bread alone; we do not really live by bread at all. Beefsteak and potatoes are not the raw materials from which life and mind are made. The old physiology is controverted by the law of the conservation of energy.

So much for our first proposition; now for the second:

Most muscle workers would be stronger, healthier and longer lived on one-half, and most brain workers on one-tenth of the food they now consume.

Since Dr. Dewey's books were published some Hundreds of thousands of people have adopted the no-breakfast plan, going entirely without food until noon; and nearly all of them have found, to their astonishment that they were stronger, brighter, and had more work power without the breakfast than with it. And the exceptions are nearly always those who cannot grasp the idea that the possession of strength does not depend on keeping the stomach full.

This it the philosophy of the no-breakfast plan:

You awake with the brain fully charged with work-power and your blood contains the tissue elements of the previous days' food; therefore in the

best possible condition for work. Why should you eat? It takes power to run the stomach; why not save the power for your other work! You are not really hungry; there is no such thing as a normal hunger on arising in the morning, in a person who has been sufficiently fed on the previous day. Your morning appetite is a matter of habit; of mental attitude You eat because you are afraid you will get faint later in the day; or you tickle your palate. with sweet foods until you arouse a taste for more; but you never eat breakfast because you are genuinely hungry.

If you do not believe all this, put it to the best possible test; try it on yourself. Get up and go to work without eating; and if you are in anything approaching a normal condition you will find that you are in better condition for mental or physical labor with an empty stomach than with a full one.

Mind, though, much depends upon your mental attitude; remember that many people who believe in the old physiology have starved to death in ten days, while others, better taught, have fasted forty days without much discomfort. If you expect that because your stomach is empty you will have a fainting fit about ten o'clock, the fainting fit will probably come; you will get just about what you look for. On the other hand, if you put the thought of food resolutely aside and go to your work without fear of any disagreeable consequences you will have a forenoon of such mental cheer, and of such physical vigor as you have seldom experienced; but you will not feel so well after your noon meal.

Why! Because you will overeat; you will mistakenly suppose that because you have done without breakfast you must eat enough, and more than enough at noon to make up the deficiency; and during the afternoon so much of your brain's energy will be required at the stomach that you will have very little left for mental or physical work. This ought to convince you that your stomach is a machine which absorbs energy, instead of being a generator for producing it. The object in dispensing with the breakfast is not to increase the quantity consumed at noon but to prevent the waste of energy in the disposition of unnecessary food. If you want to be strong, and full of snap and vigor, drop your breakfast entirely, leave off half your noon meal and two-thirds of your evening one. Eat just enough to maintain your weight; not a mouthful more. If you can hold your weight on one cracker a day and you eat two crackers the disposal of the superfluous one will be a waste of your life force; it will weaken you by just the amount of power required to dispose of it, and if you overeat as a matter of habit the surplus, will be a source of danger, disease and premature death.

You don't believe it, do you! Well, it won't cost you a cent to prove it.

If you want to have strength for your work, whether mental or physical, get eight hours of sleep every night in. a well-ventilated room; eat plain, hearty food, and the smallest quantity which will maintain your weight. If it takes power to run the stomach it is foolish to keep it in operation more than is actually necessary. "For this cause many are weak and sickly among you, and many sleep," said St Paul, writing to the Corinthians about overeating at the Lord's supper. Wise St. Paul!

Most of the dietary conclusions of the pseudo- science of medicine are based on false premises, and are therefore erroneous, and the recovery of most of the sick is greatly hindered by feeding, dating, and other interference.

Most physicians accept the theory that we can add to the strength of a sick man by inducing him to swallow food; when the fact is that every mouthful is a tax on his strength, and decreases his power of resistance. It takes power to run the stomach. In every case of severe sickness Nature takes away the appetite, because there is no power to spare for the digestive process; she wishes to conserve her energy for combat with the disease. In severe sickness Nature's way is to suspend digestion and let the brain live on the tissues of the body, which can be spared.

That is why a sick man loses in weight if you feed him, and he still loses, it is proof positive that the food is not assimilated. if it were assimilated there could be no loss in weight. And if you continue to feed under such conditions you may be absolutely certain that you are loading up his system with waste matter which must be eliminated at a fearful cost in vital power. You may lay it down as a general law which is amply proven in practice, that in the absence of appetite the patient who is fed will lose weight and strength more rapidly than the one who is not fed. When the desire for food is absent, and the tongue is heavily coated, it should be interpreted to mean; "Busy;

nothing wanted within." It is homicidal folly to feed under such conditions; the food decays in the alimentary canal, and generates poisons which are dangerous to life. No matter what the books say, it is foolish to feed the sick man whose breath tells in unmistakable language that his digestive tract is already filled with rotting filth. The sick horse will not eat; and it is to be hoped that sick men, women and children will some day be allowed by their physicians and friends to exercise horse-sense.

Nature would have the severely sick man sleep much, and not eat at all; we try to induce him to eat all he can, and we wake him every few minutes to force into his protesting stomach some nauseous: or poisonous compound of drugs. Nine-tenths of our interference

with the sick has no scientific justification, and it injurious to them, Put the sick man into a well ventilated room; make him. as comfortable as possible; shut out the neighbors, the family, the preacher, everybody but the nurse, and possibly the doctor; in most cases leave the doctor out too. It would be a great deal better if two thirds of the doctors had to resort to some other means of making a living; the other third could easily take care of all the cases where they are really needed. Give nature a chance with your sick one, and if he dies you may at least feel sure that you did not help to kill him.

The stomach is a machine which uses up power, and it is operated by power supplied from the brain, which is charged during sleep. Remember this physiological fact, and regulate your life accordingly; get sleep enough, and get it under favorable condition, and eat less.

Sleep, that knits up the ravelled sleeve of care, The death of each day's life; Balm of hurt minds, great nature's second course, Chief nourisher in life's feast.

---Shakespeare, "Macbeth"

Chapter 2 - SLEEP

He giveth His beloved sleep. --- Psalms 127: 2.

IN THE PRECEDING CHAPTER we considered some of the arguments for the new physiology, which holds that vital energy is renewed in sleep, and is not generated by the digestion of food. Man is not, as we have been taught to suppose, an engine whose power comes from the combustion of fuel, or food. If he were, be would never need rest or sleep; supplied with food he could keep on eating and working indefinitely, as an engine can work indefinitely if it is supplied with coal; Whereas; no matter how much or how often he eats, we know that he must have frequent lapses into the silence and unconsciousness of sleep in order to recharge his brain with that mysterious energy by which he lives and works.

We find by observation that the fact that vital power is received in sleep is universal with all forms of life. Men, animals, reptiles, fish and insects sleep; and plants sleep also. You will notice that I speak of vital power as being received, not generated; if the

law of the conservation of energy holds good as applied to the energy displayed by the human body, then the energy of man is received from some sources outside himself; for it is a mechanical impossibility for the organism to generate within itself the power to maintain itself, renew itself, and perform external work also. The human body cannot be regarded as being anything but a machine; and since it is found to be impossible for a machine to operate itself, and to do additional work with power generated by its own operation, I am compelled to accept the hypothesis that there is an inflow of life, which is received by all living organisms during sleep. Let me write this again, and call your attention to it for it is the greatest and most important scientific fact that has been given to the world in a century.

There is an inflow of vital power, which is received by all living organisms during sleep.

I do not know where this inflow of life comes from; I do not know whether it results from some combination of other forces or is a force which is eternally self-existent. I am simply stating the facts as I observe them, and giving the inevitable deduction from them; if the facts disprove the theories you have been holding, you will have to readjust your theories to fit the facts. It is a fact that the human body cannot possibly manufacture its on vital power and at at the same time be manufactured by its own vital power; and it is a fact that it receives its vital power in deep; and necessarily, from some source outside itself. Life comes to us from somewhere; we do not make it; we receive it. I do not say that it is received only in sleep; I do not know but that there are conditions under which we may receive it when awake. Neither do I say that we always receive it directly from the unknown source; there may be individuals who can become so charged with it as to be this to communicate it to others; I do say however, that no individual has power to create it in himself he can only give what he has received, so that ultimately we will receive from the unknown source.

Now, as to the importance of all this: Hold up your finger, and examine it carefully. What made it? It is made of different ehemical elements taken from the food you have eaten; but what combined those elements and built them into a finger, Life! You slept, and your brain was charged with power; that power was applied to the stomach and bowels and digested your food; it took the separate elements and emptied them into the blood; your heart, which beats by brain power, forced them along through the arteries until they came to the finger; and vital energy from the brain built them into bone, muscle, nerve and connective tissue. Life built the finger; and nothing can make another like it. All the science in the world cannot duplicate it; we may make something which looks very much the same, but it will not be like your finger at all. Be careful, therefore about the gentleman who tells you that he has a "remedy which will renew your finger or fix it up all right if there is anything the matter with it. Nothing can repair or renew the finger but the force which created it --- vital power. Nothing can make a finger, nothing can mend a broken or injured finger, and nothing can cure a sick finger but life. There is no remedy, and no known force that can unite a broken bone save life only; and there is no remedy and no force that can make a heart beat save life only. Nothing ever made a heart beat but life; all the other powers in the world cannot send a single pulse-throb through the arteries of a dead body. No medicine ever made your heart beat, and none ever will; nothing ever made a heart beat but vital power. The force which operates your heart is stored in your brain during sleep. The only manner in which a medicine could make your heart beat would be by causing the vital power to flow from your brain to your heart. I do not say that medicine can or cannot do this; I will touch upon this point again.

What is true of the heart is necessarily true of every other organ of the body; they are all operated by brain-power, and cannot be operated by any other power. We hear certain medicines spoken of as having power to move the bowels; but a study must convince us that the only power on earth which can move the bowels is that which is stored in the brain. If a medicine causes the bowels to move it must do so by causing the brain to move them; you understand that I do not say that it is impossible for medicine to do this; I simply say that it is impossible that it should be done in any other way. The vital power which is stored in the brain during aleep is the only power capable of producing functional action any part of the body. Your heart, stomach, liver, kidneys and bowels are not separate and independent machines operated by different and extraneous powers; they are all parts of one machine, which is run by brain-power; and the brain is charged in sleep. Now, if there is defective action, or congestion, or inflammation, or pain in any part of the body, the only possible way to effect a cure is by directing the brain-power to the affected part. If a medicine can do this it is of value, provided its benefit be not neutralized by reactionary or other effects. Local applications produce their curative effect in this manner a mustard plaster cannot increase functional action in the organs over which it is applied, but it is possible that by it a chemical effect upon the tissues may cause the brain to turn its power in that direction, and so increase functional action. This is the only theory of medical action which is in accord with the facts; and we must apply it also in explaining the effects of exercise and massage. Neither exercise nor message can build up a weak part; but. either may cause the brain to build it up, by directing its power to it. Mental healing is accomplishecl in exactly the same way; it is done by consciously and intelligently directing the brain-power by concentration of mind; and it is by far the most scientific and effective method of healing, when not complicated by speculative absurdities which befuddle the mind and prevent direct and positive action.

Now, again, perhaps you do not see the importance of all this. Go back over this chapter, and the preceding one; examine the facts and study the logic of the deductions. You will hardly fail to become convinced that your body is a machine which is operated by power which is stored in your brain during sleep; and that no other agency can heal it, build it up, or keep it well but this brain-power. If you are sick or weak you know now where your cure is to be found; and you are ready to begin to act intelligently.

First, if the power which is to heal you is to be stored in your brain during sleep, you had better study sleep, and learn how to surround yourself with favorable conditions for the charging of your storage battery with power; sleep intelligently, and with a purpose, so as to get the best results. There are laws which govern the process of charging the brain with vital force; some of them are known; enough to enable you to set to work with a reasonable certainty of getting good results.

Second, having learned how to charge your brain with vital power you must learn how to conserve the power; how to keep yourself from throwing it away, and expending it uselessly; and this is more important, perhaps, than you imagine: Most people waste at least half their vital power.

Third, you will need to learn how to turn this force to the part where it is most needed; and this involves the consideration of all medicines, treatments, exercises, and mental processes.

What we need above all else is to be scientific in our methods of arriving at conclusions. We must avoid speculation, and fanciful theories based on the supposed need for retaining old medical or religious dogmas, and stick to the facts and to the deductions which are the inevitable corollary of the facts. If the facts do not accord with the teaching of the doctor and the physiological authorities, we will have to disbelieve the doctor and the authorities, and accept the facts; and if the facts disagree with the dogmas of the preacher we will have to ask the preacher to revise his dogmas; we must keep to the facts. And here, again, are some of the facts, and some of the things which the facts prove:

In death by starvation the brain loses no weight, but is nourished at the expense of the other tissues

of the body. Death does not come so long as there are other tissues available for the brain to feed upon. This proves that the brain, not the stomach is the alpha --- the center of vital power.

The structure of the body goes to prove that the brain is the power plant; the afferent nerves carrying sensation in, and the efferent ones carrying power out. It is an absurdity to suppose that muscular power is generated by the muscles themselves; it is far more reasonable to assume that power is transmitted to them over the nerves in a manner similar to the transmission of power over an electric wire.

The strength of the body is not drawn from food; because

(a) It would be impossible to extract the amount of energy displayed by the body from the quantity of food. Consumed;

(b) Work-power does not increase in proportion to the quantity of food digested;

(c) If work-power came from food we would not be obliged to sleep for the purpose of renewing our strength; and

(d) The digestion of food is work in itself, and requires the expenditure of power; it cannot, therefore, be done with power drawn in the ultimate from its on processes. Work cannot do itself with power furnished by itself. It is a manifest impossibility that the body should work with energy manufactured by its own internal processes, which are themselves a part of its work, and consume its power.

Lastly, we see that every lining thing goes regularly to sleep, and wakes with renewed energy.

From all this we deduce:

That the external work of the human organism is done, and its internal process carried on by means of a vital energy which is accumulated in the brain during sleep.

That the vital energy is the only power by which the body may he healed, repaired, renewed or maintained.

Were I to adopt a pet idea as so many people do, and fondle it in my embraces to the exclusion of ali others, it would be, that the great want which mankind labors under at this present period is sleep,. The world should recline its vast head on the first convenient pillow and take an age-long nap. It has gone distracted through a morbid activity, and while preternaturally wide awake, is nevertheless tormented by visions that seem real to it now, but would assume their true aspect and character were all things once set right by an interval of soul repose.

---Hawthorne, "Mosses from an Old Manse"

The mind grows wiser by watching, but her sister, the body, of coarser materials, needs the support of repose, --- Scott, "Talisman"

Chapter 3 - TO USE SLEEP

HAVING SETTLED that the brain charged with vital power during sleep, the next important thing is to study the process, and see if we may arrive at any conclusion as to the laws which govern it. In observing the phenomena of sleep, the most noticeable thing is the change in the manner of breathing.

The sleeping person breathes deeply, strongly and with a more rhythmic movement than the waking one; a much larger quantity of air is taken into the system in a given time during sleep than when awake. Very few persons breathe audibly when awake, while frequently the deep, strong breathing of a sleeping person can be heard throughout a house of ordinary size. Since deep and rhythmic breathing is universal during sleep, I conclude that it ia an essential part of the process of charging the brain with vital power, and that a large quantity of air is necessary to the operation. I notice an apparent connection between air and vital power as shown by other phenomena. When i am about to undertake a heavy lift, or to perform some feat of strength, I instinctively fill my lungs with air, as if by so doing I could add to my muscular power; and if I exercise violently nature compels me to breathe with great force and rapidity, evidently needing an increased quantity of air because of the strenuous exertion. There appears, I say, to be a direct connection between air and energy. But I find that deep breathing. is not all; I cannot renew the energy of the brain by deep breathing without sleep; I must go into the silence and become unconscious. And I do not know what it is in the air that is essential to life. It is not oxygen alone, for if you put me in an atmosphere of undiluted oxygen I will die. I must have air.

It is essential, too, that the air be pure. When I sleep in a room with no ventilation. I rise in the morning unrefreshed; the battery has been very imperfectly charged. It is therefore necessary to have air which is in motion; since motion is essential: to the purity of air. It will not answer the purpose to set a spool of thread under the window and put the bed's head back in the corner, out of the "draft." The draft is just what I want to get into. The object of ventilation is to produce motion in the air, so that we can breathe air which moves. It is not enough to raise the sash well up, if that is the only opening, for the air in the center of the room, or in the corner where the bed's head stands may be absolutely motionless and stagnant and remain so throughout the night.

There is not the slightest reason for the universal. fear of drafts; a draft is air in motion, and motion does not impart any evil quality to air; on the contrary moving air is far more likely to be pure than that which is stagnant. The chemical processes by which air purifies itself depends on motion. There is no reason to suppose that cold air is dangerous; that is, if it is not so cold as to actually freeze one.

The night air is not less salubrious than day air. Night air is air with the light out of it, and taking the light out of air does not make it noxious There is no evidence to support the idea that damp air is harmful, damp air is air with a little water in it, and water is not a poison.

If you lack vitality of power and wish to proceed scientifically in charging your brain with it, you must first disabuse your mind of the notion that pure air, in any place or under any condition or in any quantity is harmful; and you must come to understand the fact that the first great necessity of life is a plentiful supply of absolutely pure air during sleep.

So, attend first to the ventilation of your sleeping room. If there is only one room in the house that can be ventilated sleep in that room no matter how inconvenient it may be otherwise. Begin by providing for a current of air across the room. Open a door or window on each side; wide open. Do not be afraid of burglars; better be carried off by a burglar than by the undertaker. When you have arranged for a current of air through the room, pull your bed out so that your head will be right in the middle of the stream. If you are not quite free from the old fear of moving air, you had better do this gradually, bringing the bed out a foot or two it a time otherwise you may scare yourself to death with your fears of the dreadful "draft!"

Now understand that no matter what your disease may be, there is only one power which can cure you. You may have consumption, typhoid fever, appendicitis, cancer, liver complaint, a broken leg or a sore toe; but the only power which can make you whole is your own vital energy. The life that is in you is all the life there is; and you must accumulate enough of it to overcome the diseased or morbid condition. And you get it in sleep, and fresh, pure, moving air is absolutely accessary to the process. Do not close the window because it is damp; breathe the pure air, water and all. Do not close the window because it is cold; pile on bed clothes or make a fire. Do not "air" your bedroom during the day and close it at night; better reverse the process. Sleep the year round with your head in a running stream of pure air, fresh from out-of-doors.

There are certain other things which are pretty well established. In a vast majority of cases eight hours is about the right length of time to pass in sleep every day. More than eight hours is too much. It is generally better to sieep six hours than ten. Don't ask me why, because I do not know.

And a condition of absolute physical and mental relaxation and positivity is demanded for the best results, It is a mistake to eat before going to bed. The digestion of food is work, and if you wish to gain strength you should not work while you are sleeping, I know, if you are mentally excited or disturbed you can often become unconscious more speedily after eating; that is because the stomach is robbing the brain of power, but unconsciousness while the brain works is not genuine sleep, and the charging process is very imperfect under such conditions; and you will lack power the next day. And you cannot make up the loss by eating more; the more you eat the weaker you will be. What you lose in sleep cannot be recovered at the table. There are better ways of curing insomnia than by overworking the stomach. Never mind what anybody tells you about the necessity for stuffing; go to bed with your stomach empty. The digestion of food is work, and you cannot have a natural, effective sleep while you are at work.

So far, you will please notice, I have written on physical energy or work power; not of will power. Will power or spiritual control is also acquired in the silence, but with this difference --- we do not become unconscious. We will talk about that in subsequent chapter, but I want to call attention here to the fact that certain thought conditions are essential to perfect sleep. A brain whose power is being drawn upon for thought cannot sleep. You cannot sleep and dream at the same time; the more you dream the less perfect is the renewal of your vital power. I do not wish you "pleasant dreams" or any other kind; I hope you may sleep.

Absolute quietude of mind; the cessation of an physical and mental activity, the relaxation which comes only with perfect trust in God, is a necessary condition for "restfull" sleep; but while this is true, there is an element of positive thought which may enter in, possibly with advantage. It is a demonstrable fact, that I will show you later, that the brain power may he directed to or withheld from any part of the body by thought; and there is pretty good evidence that the character of the last thought on going to sleep may influence the course of the brain current during the night. Those who indulge in lascivious waking dreams are apt to have lascivious sleeping dreams; and to become unduly stimulated in the sexual system by an abnormal tuning of power in that direction, I am quite sure that it is possible to turn the vital energy toward any weak or defective organ, on going to sleep; but I am not so confident as to the wisdom of this, for it seems to me that sleep is for the gathering of force, and not for its expenditure in healing, or any other activities, I would be careful about setting the mind at work to heal myself or others during sleep; the best time to think your healing thoughts is when you are awake, Suppose, when you lie down tonight you try a formula like the following.

"I have opened my window, and the pure air, filled with vital power, comes streaming in; the One Great Life is seeking to find me, and to fill me with Itself. l relax, and open my soul as I have opened my windows; I shall he filled with Life while I sleep; and it will give me power to overcome every ill and all weakness. Flow in oh, Life, and give me strength and I will use it, by the guidance of Thy love, to do Thy will. Amen."

The first wealth is health --- Emerson

Oh, thou that pinest in the imprisonment of the Actual, and creist bitterly to the Gods for a kingdom wherein to rule and create, know this of a truth, the thing thou seekest is already with thee, here or nowhere, couldst thou only see! -

-- Thomas Carlyle

Chapter 4 - Scientific Living & Healing

NOT MANY THINGS are harder to overcome than the persistent auto-suggestion that life is of material origin, and that vital power comes from food. It takes a great deal of argument to make the average man (especially if he is a woman) understand that his strength is renewed in sleep, and that he grows weaker not stronger by eating. Possibly not many of our readers are firmly grounded in this faith as yet; I shall have to argue it a little further for you, even at the risk of repeating myself.

Let me call your attention, first, to the fact that loss of appetite nearly always accompanies severe sickness. Now, if strength comes from food, why does nature "go back on us" just when we need strength most? Why does she not make the sick man ravenous with hunger, as she does the woodchopper? The latter needs food in large quantities to replace the tissues destroyed by strenuous toil; he has digestive power, and hunger is given to him. Why should not
hunger be given to the sick man, so that he can generate vital power from the food, build up his strength and get well?

The appetite is taken away in severe sickness because nature needs all her power for the work of restoring normal conditions, and there is none to spare for the labor of digestion. The digestion of food is work, and hard work; the sick man's brain has not the power for it. So nature says, "Keep out; we are busy inside; when we are ready for food we will let you know." Sick horses never eat; but sick people --- or at least their friends and physicians seldom have horse sense. When the appetite is taken away it is considered a sign that nature requires "light" foods; or that the earth should be ransacked for tempting dainties to create an appetite; whereas, nature simply wants to be let alone. Food given when the tongue is coated and the appetite gone is seldom digested; it decomposes, and the condition within the stomach of the unfortunate one becomes something horrible to think about; a putrid, poisonous mass, the dreadful odor of which can often be distinguished throughout a large apartment.

The person who fasts loses weight, but the loss all falls upon those tissues which can best be spared; and even in death by starvation, the brain and nervous system lose no weight at all.. That is, the brain eats up theother tissues; and death does not come until the skeleton condition is reached, and there is nothing more for the brain to absorb. The brain must be sustained when there is no other food it draws its nourishment from the body itself. The sick man loses in weight by just this process and it is the intention of nature that he should do so. I am not speaking of the sick man who has hunger, you understand, but of the severeiy sick one who has none. Nature desires his brain to live on its stored-up resources for a few days; she wants to economize power. And if you feed him he generally keeps right on losing weight; and the more you feed the faster he loses which is proof positive that he does not assimilate food. If he did., how could he lose weight? He lies still, and is not destroying any tissue; if he assimilated food he could not fail to gain in weight. And, I repeat, the patient who is fed generally loses weight and strength faster than the one who eats nothing at all proving that the disposition of the food is a tax on his energy. It would be as logical, and as scientific, to set the sick man chopping wood as to feed him; working his stomach is as bad for him as working his arms would be.

Even when the sickness is chronic, and there is some appetite, the greatest care should be used not to overeat. Where little or no exercise is taken, the amount of food required is very small indeed, and there is nothing to gain and everything to lose by eating more than is readily assimilated. Very, very many invalids are kept weak and low because their brain power it wasted by overeating; sick or well, if you are eating more than is required to maintain you body you are robbing yourself of vital power, and charging your system with deadly poison besides.

In cases of severe sickness, do not offer the patient food nor mention it in his presence; put him in a cool, airy room and make him as comfortable as possible; give him a chance to sleep; do not let him be talked to, or fussed over; keep out the neighbors, the doctor and the preacher; and if the disease is curable, he will get well. The scientific use (or non-use, as the case may be) of air, water, food, exercise, sleep and thought will cure any disease that is curable at all.

Be sure you do not mention food until the sick one asks for it with well developed hunger. Do not fear that he will suddenly starve to death, and drop off all in a minute when your back is turned. He will starve faster if you feed him than if you do not. Trust nature; when she is ready for food she will let you know.

If the sickness is not severe, and there is little appetite, bear in mind that the way to conserve brain power is to eat no more than is actually demanded, and that a sick person, who exercises little needs very little indeed. One egg makes a pretty fair day's ration for the average sick person --- even for one who is "up and around"; and if most of the sick who are trying to eat all they can, and racking their brains and thesis of their friends to think of "something they can eat," would cut their day's food down to one egg, or its equivalent in weight and value, they would surprise themselves and their doctors by an immediate gain in weight and strength. Save your brain power, and get strong and well.

Let us now give a little thought to the phenomena we see in the class of diseases called catarrhal --- coughs, colds, hayfevers, etc. In many cases an enormous quantity of matter is expectorated or discharged; and the question I wish to press upon you is, Where does it all come from? Clearly, nothing can come out of the body through the mouth, which has not been put into it; and as things are generally put into the body through the mouth, is it not apparent that what is blown out of the head must have gotten into the body by way of the stomach? Is it not an unavoidable conclusion that catarrhal discharges are taken from the food consumed; that they are simply food matter gone wrong? If there is a discharge from the body we know that one of two things must be true; either the tissues are breaking up and coming away, or the discharge comes from the dining tables.

This is the process. of "taking cold." A pound of food is needed in the system, and we eat, say, two pounds. Digestion being good, the whole quantity is

taken into the blood. Nature has use for only one pound, and she uses that, repairing bone, muscle and nerve. The other pound she has no use for, but it has been forced upon her, and she must dispose of it. She may deposit a little of it on the body in the form of fat, and eliminate more through the kidneys, lungs and skin; but there will still be some ounces left to decay in the blood --- for food matter will decay in the blood. So there is a little rotten matter --- sewage left in the blood as the result of that meal. At the next meal the process is repeated; and at the next, and the next. The quantity of decaying waste in the blood gets greater, until at last the arterial flow is like a stream into which the sewage of a city is emptied, foul and thick with decaying refuse, which all comes from the dining table.

At last the stream gets so thick that nature must call a halt; she cannot carry on the processes of bodily renewal with that foul blood; it must be purified. So there is a chill; a congestion in some part of the mucous membrane, and the impurities begin to be strained off. When you take cold you cough up and blow out the surplus food you have been eating; it would kill you if you did not get rid of it. The cold is an effort of nature to save your body from dissolution. it is not caused by drafts or exposure; it is caused by overeating. if you do not overeat you may drafts, or sleep in them, or expose yourself as you please, and you will. not take cold. You "catch" cold at the table; you cannot get one anywhere else. That is where we get catarrh, which is a chronic cold. A year of scientific living will cure the worst case of catarrh that ever happened, climate or no climate.

And this is the way the new physiology accounts for catarrh, and catarrhal diseases. You may easily avoid these ills if you only realize. that you do not have to stuff yourself with large quantities of food in order to generate vital power. Your life is more than meat It is not drawn from material things, and food does not contribute to life or strength in any way. You need food only to supply the spirit with material from. which to construct a body, and the quantity required is very, very much less than most of you have believed.

Let us talk a little now about "germ" diseases. The people.
of the city of Chicago have dug greet tunnels out under the
lake a mile or so, to get pure water. They want to get far
away from the water of the river, which is thick. with
rotting sewage, like the blood of a glutton. There are plenty
of disease germs in the river, but none out in the lake;
disease germs cannot live and propagate in water which
does not contain sewage; and it is also a fact that they
cannot propagate in blood which does not contain sewage.
If your blood it like the pure water of Lake Michigan no
disease germ can live in it; but if it is like the Chicago river
it will be a breeding ground for any organism that may be
introduced into it. This is bed-rock, scientific fact. If your
blood. is pure you are. immune to germ disease; you cannot
have typhoid, la grippe, smallpox or diptheria nor can you
catch cold. Disease germs can only propagate in impure
blood, and blood is made impure by overeating, and by not
breathing enough.

How much more sensible and scientific to purify the stream
than to try to neutralize the germs by loathsome counter-
poisons!

Let me close this chapter outlining a sane regime of living.,
We do not need food on arising in the morning. We have
slept, and the brain is fully charged with power; there is no
demand for food, for there has been no destruction of
tissues. No one is really hungry in the morning; the appetite
for breakfast in a forced and unnatural one. Most people do
not eat breakfast because they are hungry, but for fear of
collapse later in the day; they think to store up energy in
the stomach against a future need. Drop off the breakfast
altogether, and as soon as you get your mind adjusted to the
plan you will find that no matter whether your work is
mental or physical you can do more of it "on an empty

stomach" and do it better. At noon, eat a moderate meal of any plain hearty food that your taste may call for and eat a very light supper between six and seven o'clock. If you are a brain worker, make your dinner very light also; by "light" I mean small in quantity, not of chaffy nutterieis. Do not bother your head about carbohydrates and nitrogens; eat what you like best. The invalid and the brain worker need exactly the same foods that the woodchopper needs, but not nearly so much. Your taste is the safest guide as to what you shall eat; let it be beans, potatoes, sauerkraut, hog and hominy --- anything that will stay on a Christian stomach, if you desire it, but not too much! And above all things, never eat when you are not hungry.

Life is an energy which is stored in the brain during sleep. If we understand that material food plays no part in the generation of this energy, and govern our appetites accordingly, we shall have perfeet health. If we live according to the simple law of life no material thing an harm us. We are spiritual beings; we get our life in the Great Silence, out of which we came. We shall live after we cease to eat, for we do not live by eating now; our physical bodies are kept up by a mysterious power which comes to us while we are unconscious. God is Spirit; and He giveth life to all.

It is notorious that a single successful effort of moral volition, such as saying "No" to some habitual temptation, or performing some courageous act, will launch a man on a higher level of energy for days and weeks, will give him a new range of power. The emotions and excitements due to usual situations are the usual inciters of the will. But then act discontinuously; and in the intervals the shallower levels of life tend to close in and shut us off. Accordingly the best knowers of the human soul have invented the thing known as methodical, ascetic discipline to keep the deeper levels constantly in reach. Beginning with easy tasks, passing to harder ones and exercising day by day, it is, I believe, admitted that disciples of asceticism am reach very high levels of freedom and power of will. Ignatius Loyola's spiritual exercises must have producd this result in innumerable devotees; But the most venerable ascetic system, and the one whose results have the most voluminous, experimental corroboration is undoubtedly the Yoga system in Hindustan.

--- William James, "Energies of Man"

Chapter 5 - MIND CURES

IN THE SECOND CHAPTER I asserted that nothing can repair, restore, heal or renew the body or any part of it but vital power --- the energy which is stored in the brain during sleep. Nothing but brain power, conducted to . it over the "motor" nerves, can make a heart beat; and nothing but brain power can "strengthen" a weak heart. Nothing but brain power can cause a liver to secrete bile; and a "torpid" liver is one to which the brain power is imperfectly conducted or applied. Nothing but brain power can cause a movement of the bowels; the only power which can cure constipation is that which is stored in the brain during sleep. This is pretty hard for you to believe, if you have been taking medicines to "strengthen" your heart, "act" on your liver, and "move" your bowels; but it is a demonstrable scientific fact nevertheless. How much medicine will It take to make a dead man's heart beat, his liver act or his bowels move? Can medicine move heart, liver or bowels when the brain is not charged with life? The most that can be said of medicine is that it (or the belief in it,) causes the brain power to be applied to certain parte of organs. You must understand that your liver like every other organ of your body is built and planned to be operated by brain power; it cannot be operated by medicine, or by anything else, any more than an electric motor can be made to run by turning a steam jet against it. The electric motor is only built to be run by one kind of power; and the same is true of the liver. There is not the slightest evidence that there is any "remedy" which can "act" on the liver, or cause the liver to act; and this is true of all the viscera.

How, then, do we get effects from medicine! Let me show you. Suppose I begin to write here a detailed description of things good to eat --- fried chicken, lemon pie strawberries and cream --- yum, yum! You read a little way, and you notice an increased flow of saliva into your mouth; it "makes your mouth water." How can. the thought of strawberries and cream cause the saliva to flow! Only by causing the brain power to be turned on; nothing but brain power an cause the salivary glands to act. Tickle the inside of the mouth with s straw and the saliva will flow; why? Because the afferent nerves carry the irritation to the brain and cause the power to be turned on. The power is turned on to the whole digestive system by the thought eating.; and it is withheld by anxiety, or the fear of indigestion; but this another story, which I will tell you a little farther on.

Suppose, instead of strawberries. and cream, I tell you of something horrible and disgusting, --- say a dead cat. Pretty soon you begin to be nauseated; and you may even vomit. How can the thought of a dead cat cause vomiting? Only by causing the brain power to be turned on to the stomach with that intention; and that is the only way an emetic can produce its effect. Nothing but the brain can cause vomiting; an emetlc introduced into a dead man's stomach lies inert and powerless. Some emetics act through belief only; others, perhaps, irritate the sensory nerves of the stomach in such a way as to cause the power to be turned on; but it is always the brain which really empties the stomach.

Of course there are medicines which set directly on the parts with which they come in contact --- corrosive chemicals which effect the lining membranes of the alimentary canal. These ought never to be taken, and the ignorance which prescribes them is homicidal. Irritation of the sensory nerves, in any part of the body, causes the power to be turned on in. that direction. That, as I have mentioned in a previous chapter, explains the action of all "strengthening," "soothing," "healing" and other applications. A mustard plaster has no power to increase action in the parts beneath it; but its irritation causes the brain to act.

Liniments, etc, cannot overcome morbid conditions; but by reflex action or by the patient's faith, they may cause the direction of an increased amount of brain power to the affected part. And there is not the slightest evidence that medicines do or can "act" except as described above.

What I say of medicine applies also to massage and exercise. Massage may shake and work loose the obstructions to the circulation in a congested tissue; and it may cause the brain power to be turned on. It cannot increase "local action" because, strictly speaking, there is no local action; all action is from the brain. Shaking and pounding a torpid liver, loosens the morbid matter in the ducts and channels and draws power from the brain to move the matter on; but it does not cause the liver to act, for the liver never acts; the brain acts through it. This ought to be understood in applying massage: That there are two things to accomplish, the through loosening of the tissues and opening of the channels and the turning on of power of the brain. Massage cannot "build up" a weak or defective part; only brain power can do that. This is also true of exercise, Exercise does not strengthen weak parts; the brain does that. Exercise does not make big muscles; the brain does that also! Don't fly off the handle, you physical culture enthusiast; let me explain. How do you build up a weak part by exercise, Flex and relax the biceps muscles vigorously for a few momenta; the quantity of blood flowing to it is greatly increased, and the blood carries the food; the muscle is fed more just in proportion it is used more, and it grows larger and thicker. The benefit of exercise is that it turns the brain power to the part you wish to build; and with brain power goes an increased blood supply, which carries the nourishment So it is the brain which makes the big muscles, you see. Exercise really tears a part down, and the brain restores it. And let me give you a gentle hint right here. If the above is true --- and if surely exercise is not beneficial to a sick man, but only those movements which direct the power to the afflicted part. If your back is weak and you take arm and leg exercises, you are drawing power away from the part you wish to help; that is the reason why "physical culture courses" under the guidance of pugilists and ex-champion wrestlers are as apt to do the sick harm as to do them good, For a weak back, take ten minutes night and morning of exercise which uses the muscles in the weak place; and do not neutralize the effect by going through other movements which draw the power to other parts of the body. Remember that ten minutes twice a day is worth more than two hours at irregular intervals; what you want to do is to regularly, systematically and continuously demand of the brain that a little more power and nourishment be sent to the weak part. That is the way to exercise scientifically for curative effect. Ask, and keep on asking, and ye shall receive.

That is you will receive if you put your mind into the demand. And now we erree at the crux of this whole healing business. Neither medicine, massage nor exercise can produce effect if opposed by the mind of the patient I hope you will read and consider carefully what follows. It is the most important of all, so far.

Let a person be laid on his back on a bed, accurately balanced so that the bead and foot may swing up and down; now let him be asked to perform severe mental labor, and the bed's head will tip down, because of an increased flow of blood to his head. Let him go through a series of leg exercises and the foot of the bed will tip down, because of the increased now of blood to the legs, and mark! Let him think out the leg exercises, without moving a muscle, and the foot will go down., showing that it is the intention to move which sends the blood to the legs; and if the intention is formed in the mind, the power goes whether the movement is really executed or not. It is the thought of exercise, and not really the exercise whkh. sends the blood to the muscle; and if the thought be withheld the exercise accomplishes next to nothing as a building process. That is why exercise which is taken under compulsion, which is a drag and a task, does no good. That is why mere muscular toil and drudgery rarely make strong men and women., but generally makes weaker ones. Work or exercise. to be beneficial must be done freely, joyously and confidently; if it be mechanical and automatic it is useless expenditure of power, and tears down. instead of building up.

And if the positive thought of action can send power and nourishment to the muscles of the legs, it necessarily follows that the same must be true of all parts and organs of the body. The firm, steady concentration of thought upon the "torpid" liver with the positive will and purpose to make it "go" will certainly cause action where action is possible at all. This is true of all cases of arrested action, unless there is some mechanical obstruction which requires massage, manipulation or surgery. if there is a part of the machine which isn't working, turn on the power by steady, concentrated, purposeful thought; understand that you possess at all times the power to control and direct your own vital power. And if there is a thought that turns on the power, so there must be thoughts that shut it off; and this we find by experiment to be true also. Fear or anxiety instantly arrests action. if you think of your liver with fear you off the power from it; if you think of your stomach with anxiety you deprive it of energy; if you think with fear or anxiety of the bowels you paralyze them. In most cases of constipation the cause is entirely in a habit of mind or thought which withholds power from the bowels. All cases of indigestion are greatly aggravated by anxious thought about the digestibility of foods. When you begin to worry about what you shall eat you begin to have dyspepsia, Don't think about the values of digestibility of different foods; eat what tastes good to you, but only eat from one-fifth to one-sixteenth, of what your friends would like to have you eat. That is all that is necessary to cure stomach trouble. We hear it said of melancholy people that they have the blues because their livers are bad; that is generally the reverse of the truth; their livers are bad because they have the blues.

Remember that the calm, confident, porposeful thought of faith sends the life power flowing out; and the fear thought locks it in. And can we cultivate power to think the thoughts of faith and cheer, and avoid those of anxiety, fear and discouragement! Yes, and that will be the subject for a subsequent chapter of this series.

Every man has experienced how feelings which end in themselves and do not express themselves in action, leaves the heart debilitated. We get feeble and sickly in character when we feel keenly, and cannot do the thing we feel.

–Robertson

The flighty purpose never is o'erlook, Unless the deed go with it; from this moment The very firstlings of my heart shall be The firstlings of my hands.

No boasting like a fool; This deed I'll do before the purpose cool.

--- Shakespeare, "Macbeth"

Chapter 6 - Nature and Development of Will Power

"Burnt offerings for sin thou wouldst not. Lo, I come to do thy will, Oh, God!" --- Heb. X: 8-9

ON HUMAN LIFE I seem to see three different forms of manifestations of energy, which for convenience's sake. I am going in this article to call physical, mental, and spiritual. Physical energy is what we have been treating of in this series of articles; proving that it is not drawn from food, but is received in sleep. It is the life force of the organism, the work power of the body. Mental energy is thought power. I do not know what the difference between physical work power and thought power may be; I do not know whether there is a difference or not; but I know that there are individuals who have a great deal of physical power and apparently very little thought power; and there are others who have a great deal of thought power and very little vital energy; and so I will consider them as separate forms of force. We will, therefore, adopt this hypothesis; that you display three forms of energy; first, the physical power, which carries on the work of the material body, and second, the power which runs your think-machine. I do not know what your think machine is, or where it is; I do not know whether you think with your brain or not; I am inclined to think that you do not; but anyway, I know that you have a thinker, because you think; and I know that it takes power to operate your thinker, because thought is a force itself, and cannot be produced without the expenditure of force. So I know that you have a thinker and that it takes power to run it; and I am assuming that this power is different from physical energy, although I do not know that it is; but it makes my point a little clearer to speak of physical energy and thought power as if they were diffennt things.

Now, this thinker of yours is absolutely indifferent to moral considerations. It knows nothing, and cares nothing about good and evil. There is no connection between thought power and goodness. Bad people often have much thought power, and many excellent souls have very little. A devil may be a very keen and acute thinker, and a saint may be almost destitute of reasoning power. Your thinking machine works in the direction in which you set it running. If you start it planning to execute a noble deed of charity, it will go on we arrange all the details, and if you put it at work on a plan to rob a bank, it will work on the details of that plan just as readily. I think you will agree with me, however, that you have, at least in a rudimentary way, the power to control and direct your think-machine. You tell it to think about this, and it does; or to cease thinking about this, and to consider that, and it obeys you. So you see here are the three forms of power I have mentioned --- first, physical power; second, thought power, and third, the power to control and direct the thought

Now, it is this power to control and direct the think-machine that we wish to develop. The trouble it that there are too many other forces operating it Some one, or some thing, starts it running on the fear thought or the thought of despondency and discouragement, and it runs away from us; we want to master it completely, so that it will only work on the thoughts of hope and faith and love and health; how to do it is the question; how to develop this power of control. For it is not a thing to be acquired, but one to be developed; we have it within.

Did your thinking machine ever run away with you along the line of self pity? First, it says, you are not appreciated; you are not understood; those around you do not realizer how fine your nature is, and how delicate your sensibilities are! They are all blind, callous, selfish; they do not love you as they ought, they do. not see, or seem to care how they make you suffer! Ah well, they will be sorry, when it is too late! And then your imagination runs on and you see yourself sick, dying, dead --- and your weeping friends stricken with awful remorse, standing around your coffin and wishing they had treated you better --- how did your thinker get get started on that line? And when it reached a certain point did not something else seem to rise up within you and say; "Nonsense! You know better than all this! Stop it, and think sense" It was as if the engine ran away while the engineer slept, and he suddenly awakened and assumed control. This engineer is always within you. You have always faith and hope and love at the center of your being. You do not have to acquire them from without, but to arouse them within. The engineer is there, but he is like one in a tomb, asleep; he must hear the voice and come forth. That is salvation. "You who were dead in trespasses and sins hath he quickened.," said St. Paul, who was very scientific. To be dead in trespasses and sins is simply to have lost control of your thinker. The engineer is in a dead deep, and the sin thought and the fear thought and the disease thought are running the engine. The force works undirected. How shall we waken the engineer, and get him "quickened" so he will stay awake! How shall we vitalize this third principle, and get the power of control over our own internal forces.This is the supreme question. We Know how to charge the battery of vital power in sleep; how shall we energise the soul?

Let me point you to the connection between silence and physical power. When you want vital energy you have to quit reaching, snatching, and grabbing for it, and just lie and shut your eyes and let it come. To charge the brain with power you must get still; stop the busy hand, close the eyes, suspend the action of the senses; and life comes in. Cease all activities, and couple on to the one Eternal Life as to a dynamo, and get charged. That is the process. Why not try it in charging the will! Suspend all other work and make connection with the Eternal Will, and receive Spiritual power as we receive physical energy; why not!

I wonder if any of our readers were ever in an old-fashioned Quaker meeting, where the congregation sat in silence for an hour? If you were, you know something of how it feels to be in an atmosphere surcharged with spiritual power. For a hundred devout men and women to sit together in perfect silence for an hour, with their thoughts withdrawn from earthly things and their souls open toward God --- it is no wonder that the any Quakers were spiritual giants and giantesses. it is a great pity that the friends of the present day have fallen in line with the practices of their competitors and fill every moment of their meetings with gibble, gabble. gobble --- words, words, words! The marked spiritual power which once distinguished the Quakers came to them in their silent meetings, and they have lost it with the discontinuance of the practice. The silent meeting was scientific; it was in line with the law of transmission of life, and to that law you must individually conform if you are to have energy of soul.

So, this is the method. Go into yourr closet and. shut the door. Get by yourself in the quietest place you can find, and where you may be free from interruption for a little while.

And sit down; relax the body; rest. And now, stop thinking. You have not gone apart to meditate, or to think about God, or about anything else. Stop thinking; silence; be still. And when you are still begin to pray. Now this is s wordless prayer, and a prayer without thought. You are not to pray with the thinking-machine but with the will. You are not to think thoughts and tell them to God; nor are you to ask Him to think thoughts and tell them to you. You are not seeking God's thoughts but His energy. You do not wish to hitch your thinker to His thinker, but to unite your will to His will. You will readily see that if there is a purpose in the universe, there must also be a will behind the purpose, and this will must be the source of all will power. Get rid of the notion that there is any connection or similarity between stubborness and will power. Will power is power to control and direct your own thought. It is spiritual energy and comes by connection with the universal will, in like manner as physical energy comes by connection with One Life.

What manner of prayer then will connect your will with the will of God! Only this, and no other

"I will to do Thy will, oh God!"

That is all the prayer you need. "Not every man that sayeth unto me Lord, Lord, but be that willeth to do the will of my Father shall enter the Kingdom." To will to do the will of God is the sum of all religion. It is the highest possible assertion of selfhood. It comprehends all possible good effort, and shuts off all evil. It suspends all activity but God's and holds the soul in silence before him. It is the greatest assertion of will power of which man is capable. Angels can do no more. And that within you which wills to do the will of God is the power which can direct and control your thought. Exercise it; call it into activity. Sit in the silence and hold your soul on the will to do the will of God. When you cannot or do not wish to concentrate longer, arise and go out. Do this every day or twice a day; and whenever your thinker gets beyond your control for an instant, will to do the will of God. You will, find yourself in the way of power and life; you will draw spiritual power from God in the silence by day as you draw vital energy from Him in the silence of night.

"For I do not my own will, but the will of Him that sent me."

"Not my will, but thine."

"I do always His will."

That, beloved, is the way to get will power; and will power is the spiritual ability to control and direct yourself in thought and deed, internal and external.

And now, here are the conclusions:

Never eat unless you are hungry.

If you. are a hard worker or a young person, eat two moderate meals a day,

if a brain worker, an invalid or an old person, eat only one meal and not much at that.

Sleep in pure air.

Think good thoughts.

And acquire power to do all these things by willing to do the will of God.

Chapter 7 - The Living One

AT THE RISK of being guilty of wearisome repetition, I
must here re-state some of the things. which have gone,
before. I want you to, have them. fresh in your mind, so
that you will fully grasp the arguments which follow for the
point is one which is rather difficult to state. Life is a force,
a form of energy, as truly as heat and electricity are forms
of energy. That which performs work is force, or energy.
There is no distinction to be made between the life of the
body and its work-power. Life is work-power, The work-
power of the body is most drawn from the food consumed;
this we have proved by the following facts:

1. The anatomical structure of the body, which proves
that the brain, not the stomach, is the powerplant of the
organism.

2. The phenomena of sleep prove that the brain is
charged with work-power during the period of sleep.

3. It is a mechanical impossibility that the enormous
amount of work-power displayed by the body should be in
the food consumed, A handful of rice cannot possibly
furnish power to carry two hundred pounds over twenty
miles of rocky ground.

4. People can fast, if properly instructed, from twenty to
sixty days without material loss of strength. This would be
impossible if the work-power were drawn from the daily
food.

5. In death by starvation the brain loses no weight.
Nature preserves the power-plant intact until the last.

6. The accession of strength felt after eating must come from the brain. It cannot come from the food, which is still an undigested mass in the stomach

7. In severe sickness Nature always takes away the appetite; proving that the digestion of food is work; a tax on strength, and not a source of strength.

8. All the other phenomena of life point us irresistibly to the conclusion that food is merely raw material, to be used in building up the body, and that it is used by an energy which is stored up in the brain during sleep.

Now, as a form of energy, life presents one peculiar characteristic; it. seems to be an exception to the: law of the correlation of forces, Heat, light, and electricity are convertible, each into the others; but none of them, so far. as we know, is convertible into life Every living thing came from a germ, which contained part of a preceding life, and contained it as life, and not as something else to be converted into life. Life only comes from life; we cannot originate, generate or create it is we do electricity, by changing or combining other forces. It does not appear, so far as our observation goes, that there was ever any new life, or that life has ever come into existence where there was none before. We with all our wisdom, skill and science, can only watch life reproduce itself; we cannot originate it.

It is the work-power of the life in the seed germ which produces the organism it is the function of life to produce organisms. The life in the seed produces the plant; the plant does not produce the life. Life is not a result of organization, but is the cause of it. Living organisms are not machines which generate life; they are machines which are built and operated by life. Life is not the result of functional. action, because it is the cause of functional action; it cannot be at once the effect and the cause. The external work of the body, as i have shown in a preceding chapter, cannot possibly be performed by power which is generated by its internal work; for the power which does both the internal and the external work is one and the same. There is no difference between the power which does muscular work and that which operates the heart, liver and stomach. It is all one, and comes from one source. It is, therefore, in absurdity to say that the work-power of the body is the, result of the performance of its internal digestive or other functions.

Life is the cause of all function,, including the digestion of food, and cannot be the result of that which it causes. We are therefore driven to the conclusion that the body receives its power from some external source. It certainly expends energy, we have seen that it does not and cannot generate this energy; it must, occasionally, be charged anew, And when we witness the phenomena of sleep we conclude that we are witnessing the vitalizing procees; the sleeping organism is being charged with power.

But where does the power come from? Oxygen, as we have seen, is necessary to the charging process, but oxygen is not life. It is a chemical element indispensable to functional action, and to the operations of vital power, but it is not life. Nor does it appear that there is any possible combination. or recombination of the elements of the atmosphere with those of the body which can produce life. For if life be drawn by chemical processes from atmospheric air, it can only be done by internal functional processes:, and we have seen that it is a mechanical impossibility that life should be the result of functional action. It is as impossible that the body should manufacture life out of air as that it should manufacture it out of food. All the arguments which, I have used in the one case will apply in the other. If vital power cannot be received by the body in the form of potential energy in food, and converted into life by functional action, then it cannot be received in the form of electrical or other energy from the atmosphere, and converted into work-power by emotional action. It must, therefore, be received directly as vital power, for the body is not a generator or transformer of energy. When the body receives life it must receive life; it cannot receive something else which is to be converted into life, for this would make life to be its own creator, the effect becoming its own cause.

Therefore, life is not drawn from the atmosphere, for the atmosphere is a compound of dead gases, It it not drawn from the earth, for the earth is dead mineral, vegetable and animal matter. There are forms of potential and kinetic energy in both earth and air-heat and electricity, for instance --- but as I have shown you, these are not life, and it is not mechanically possible for the body to convert them into life. If there is life in the air it must be there is life, and not as something else; and it must be in the air, not of the air. If there is vital power in the earth, it must be there as life, and not as some other form of force; it must be a force separate and distinct from all other forces, and not an inherent property of matter. For, if life were inherent in all matter, death and disintegration would be impossible, The body without the spirit would not be dead, but just as much alive as ever. We cannot escape the conclusion that vital power, or life, is seen by us only in the bodies of living organisms; whatever forces we see in dead matter are not alive, nor capable of being alive; for we receive life, not something else. If vital power is present in our material environment it is there as a living force --- a living presence, a life not as a dead material force, which we must convert into life in order to live.

There is one other supposition which we must consider briefly here, which is that life comes from the sun. This idea probably originated from observing the phenomena of the seasons; the forthputting of life in the spring, when the suns rays penetrate air and soil, creating the right chemical condition for the building of organisms by life. There is no evidence however, that the life of the springtime comes from the sun. A certain amount of heat is necessary to the constructive processes of vital power, but heat in excess is destructive to all the work of life. Life does not come from fire, or work in fire, or with fire and the. sun, so far as we know, is pure fire. It is unthinkable that there should, be life on, or in the sun.And so far as the facts go, life only comes from life. If there are to germs of life in the sun, then reasoning from the facts of life as I see them, I cannot accept the theory that life comes from a body where there is no life.

Whence, then, does life come! I do not know. I can only say with Swedenborg that there appears to be an inflow of life into the world, which is received by all living things according to their forms: or I can say with St. Paul that there Is a Living One in whom we live and move, and whose offspring we are. But this I know by all the laws of force, that we must get our life from a living force which surrounds us. There is no escaping this conclusion. It is mechanically impossible that we should generate life, or that we should convert some other force into it; we receive it as life, and we receive it from life.

Do you remember what happens on the window pane on a cold morning when a fire is kindled? The pane acts as a condenser, changing the form of the moisture in the air; it becomes tangible, Wherever heat and cold, positive and negative, come into contact there is a precipitation. The surface of the brain is this point of contact between positve and negative, Uncreate and Create, Spirit and Matter The positive ever acts upon at negative; the higher and finer forces upon the lower or coarser. The natural attitude of man is one of aspiration toward the Uncreate and command toward the Create; negative to the Highest positive to all beneath.

---Elizabeth Towne, in "Constitution of Man" (1898)

Chapter 8 - New Light on Immortality

FINALLY, in the light of ail the foregoing, what about the immortality of the individual? Well, the new physiology gives us, for the first time, a really scientific basis for the hope of a continued existence. You must remember that if the old physiology is true, immortality is simply impossible. If you get your vital power from food, then your soul comes from the beef trust; and when you cease to eat, that will be the end of you for time and eternity. The theory that the soul draws its vital power from God, while the body gets energy from corned beef and cabbage, is unprovable; all the evidence goes to show that there are not two kinds of life, one of the body and one of the soul, but that there is only one life. The life of the soul and the life of the body are one, and come from the same source; therefore, if the old physiology is true, the death of the body is the end of all.

To prove individual immortality we must demonstrate two things to be true:

First, that there is a spiritual organism which the ego, or individual intelligence can inhabit after the dissolution of the physical body; and

Second, that the ego can and will keep the spiritual organism so in harmony with the constructive principle of nature that it, in turn, shall not be dissolved.

It is unthinkable that life should continue individualized without an organism. There must be a separate organism. for, every individual life; and when the life can no longer preserve its organism against the attacks of nature's destructive principle, then it must cease to be an individual life, and be merged into that Universal from whence it came. What evidence have we that there are spiritual bodies?

1. We hays the testimony of clairvoyants and other psychics who claim to see them. Take this evidence for what it is worth to you. Personally, I believe some of it.

2. We are able to demonstrate mathematically that personality is not, the result of functioning of the physical body. Mind is not produced by the physical body, for mind controls the physical body. Mind is not the result of functional action, for mind can and does control functional action. There is no organ of the body whose action is not controllable by mind, properly applied, To have mind control the machinery which produces it would be to make the effect become its own cause. If mind were the result of functional action, it could. not cause or control functional action. There is no more evidence that the brain thinks that there is that the heart thinks, or that the liver thinks; the most we can say is that the brain appears to be the organ through which the ego applies thought to the physical body. It does not appear to be at all impossible that there is a spiritual organism, formed of finer material in and through the physical body, permeating it as ether permeates the atmospheric air; and that this spiritual body may continue to exist after the dissolution of the physical body.

But its continued existence must depend upon its power and willingness to co-operate with the constructive principle in nature. Look where we will, we see two principles in operation; all about us are the phenomena of construction and destruction, integration and disintegration, combination and dissolution, growth and decay, life and death. In our own bodies construction and destruction are continuous; and the length of physical life depends upon our living, so that the process of construction shall equal or exceed that of destruction. In the very nature of things, it is not possible that there should be any such thing as essential, inherent and intrinsic immortality for any living organism. Every living thing, whether spiritual or physical, must be subject to the same fundamental laws; and each must receive its vital energy from the same source. You know that you are not necessarily and inherently immortal, in so far as your physical body is concerned. You may have a long and merry life, or a short and miserable one; just as you choose.

If you eat and drink and sleep and think in a constructive way, you will live a good while --- I cannot undertake to say how long. You may achieve physical immortality, for all I can prove to the contrary, although I do not believe you can; and I do not know why you should want to unless you are afraid to pass out and try the other plane. On the other hand, if you eat and drink so as to turn your constructive force into the destructive channel; if you do not give the constructive principle an opportunity by sleeping under proper conditions, or if you think destructively, you can commit physical suicide in a very little while, or you can prolong the process over a number of years,. but it will be suicide all the same.

Permit me now to point out that the same must be true of your spiritual body. I believe that you have a spiritual body, for the reasons given above, and because I see phenomena in your life which I cannot possibly account for on any other hypothesis than that there is a personality which uses your brain but which is not produced by your brain. All that, however, is another story, and I shall not go into it now. But you will note now that it can be no more a necessity that your spiritual body shall live forever than it is that your physical body shall live forever. You are endowed with the power to commit physical. suicide, and it necessarily follows that you must also have the power to commit spiritual suicide. The spiritual bodies of those who persist in thinking the destructive thought and living in the destructive way must eventually be dissolved into their original elements, and the life principle be merged into that Universal life from whence it came. They who persist in violation of the law must eventually vanish from the universe; the. "soul that sinneth, it shall die."

Immortality is a privilege, but not a necessity. Conscious individual existence on either the physical or spiritual planes can be long continued only by working in harmony with the constructive principle; by intelligent and continuous co-operation with God. And this is the great stern fact that underlies the New Physiology: That the individual cannot create or renew his own life, or vital power of soul or body; he must, therefore, so harmonize himself with the source of life as to receive from it, or he will inevitably perish.

How wonderful is Death!

Death and his brother, Sleep.

---Percy Bysshe Shelley

Everything in nature contains all the powers of nature.

Everything is made of one hidden stuff.

--- Emerson

Chapter 9 - Suffering in Sickness

MY ATTENTION has lately been called to the case of an old lady --- seventy-six years old --- who is suffering from a severe attack of asthma, complicated with la grippe. Her sufferings are distressing to witness. She coughs almost continuously, especially during the night., and expectorates vast quantities of mucous; there is much retching and straining in the desperate efforts nature is making to eliminate this filth from the overburdened system.

Now this old lady belongs to that vast army of excellent women whose greatest pleasure is to feed their families, their visitors and themselves. It is not an exaggeration to say that most of her life has been spent in cooking, in eating and in thinking of eating, and in planning and preparing for meals When she was younger, an active and hard working housewife, she ate heartily, and with some reason, because of her physical activities; but for some years now she has done very little work, and she has gone on eating, just the same. I do not know that she has eaten less than during her year of active life. She thinks and talks continuously of eating, and of things good to eat; she frequently munches apples, etc, between meals; and she "lunches" at all hours, and often at bed time. And for some years she has suffered intensely with rheumatism, asthma, and frequently recurring attacks of the grippe.

It is impossible to make her believe that all her sufferings are caused by the terrible struggle her physical organism is compelled to make to rid itself of the filth with which she is continually gorging it; but such is actually the case. And the same is true of nearly all old people who suffer from the so-called infirmities of age. It has been said that when a man "retires" nature usually retires him permanently in a very short time; but the fact is that he usually destroys himself by continuing to eat as if he were still at work. Professor Metchnikoff discovered that old age is caused by germ which originates in putrefying matter in the intestinal tract; and he hit on the marvelously scientific scheme of drinking sour milk to kill the bad germs, as the sour milk germ is an enemy to the old-age germ. And by the way, what has become of the professor's great "discovery" that drinking plenty of sour milk would make us all immortal in body! Like most of the medical discoveries it seems to have fallen flat. It is about time for some other great "scientist" to come out with an elixir of life. Instead of trying to find a counter-poison for the old age bug why did not Metchnikoff simply advise people to eat less, so as to have no putrefying filth in the intestines! This was the plan followed by Lewis Cornaro, the feeble Italian, who lived to pass the century mark, often subsisting a whole day on half an egg, or a single bunch of grapes, And Cornaro, a broken down wreck it middle life, recovered his health and lived and died without suffering. There is no reason in nature why there should be aches and pains and physical miseries attendant upon old age; it ought to be a period of physical rest and wholesomeness, and mental cheer and joy; and the reason why it is not is generally to be told in one word --- overeating! The old lady mentioned above is very cross and crabbed; hating everybody, and disliked by most of those around her, she leads a loveless and wretched life; her vital power is so fully expended in eliminating the filth she continually shovels into her stomach that she has no strength to expend in loving people. And even in her misery, her whole thought is of something to eat. It is the first thing on awakening in the morning and it is referred to hourly during the day. "Isn't there something I can eat! Get me a little of this, or that" and so on. The poor thing eats enough to supply the needs of a hard-working man, and lingers on in excruciating torments while her enfeebled system tries to rid itself of the poisonous accumulating filth.

Another neighbor of mine, also an aged woman, passed out the other day. This was a similar case. She, also, was "a great sufferer." For weeks before she died her continuous groans and screams were heard by the neighbors; she ate three or four meals during the day, and was also fed at four o'clock in the morning. She was a heavy woman; she could have lived through the entire period of sickness without food and had she done so she would have lost less in weight, for her system would have been spared the dreadful labor of eliminating unused food; and not only would she have lost less flesh but she would have had a painless illness, and an easy death. Most of the agonies of all kinds of sickness are due to feeding.

Five years ago I was asked to advise a young man who was in the last stage of tuberculosis, with the end very near at hand. Surrounded by loving friends, who, unable to think of any other way to show their sympathy, were continually forcing food upon him, he was coughing his life away, and suffering severely in the struggle of his feeble body to eliminate the filth. I said to him: "My boy, if you want to spend your remaining days in peace and comfort, do not eat except when you are decidedly and unmistakably hungry," and I gave his family a lecture on the difference between selfish and unselfish love. That young man never ate another mouthful of food. In a few days his coughing and expectorating ceased; he slept well, and was free from pain; he became bright and cheerful, and four weeks later, he fell asleep, like a little child. In my last illness, may I be delivered from the love that feeds!

And that is about all, dearly beloved. Most of the suffering in sickness is caused by feeding the sick. Oh, I know! You don't believe any such stuff! But you try it, and see. When you are sick, stop eating. Do not think about eating; do not talk about eating; ask your friends to kindly refrain, from talking about eating; and wait until you are sure you are hungry; and then wait a few hours to make sure you are sure; and then eat enough to satisfy your hunger, and then wait again. And if you are getting along in years, and especially if you have quit work, remember that it takes only a very little raw material to maintain the body of an old person who does not work. Find out the least quantity of food upon which you can live and keep up your weight, and live on that. If you can live on one bunch of grapes, or half an egg a day, and be well and free from aches and pains, and also be bright and happy, is not that better than to eat forty bunches of grapes or a couple of dozen eggs, and be a wretched, suffering invalid, a burden to yourself and a trial to your friends!

And, by the way, this applies as well to you who are not growing old; find out the smallest quantity of food upon which you can live and work without losing weight and live on it!

Printed in Great Britain
by Amazon

44549070R00046